MOTORCYCLE ROAD RACING

MOTORCYCLE ROAD RACING

The 1950s In Photographs

Denis Jenkinson

Foreword by Geoff Duke, O.B.E.

Aston

Published in 1989 by **Aston Publications Limited,**
Bourne End House, Harvest Hill, Bourne End, Bucks SL8 5JJ

© Copyright Denis Jenkinson 1989

ISBN 0 946627 37 1

Designed by Chris Hand,

Printed in England by Oxford University Press

Sole distributors to the UK book trade
Springfield Books Ltd
Norman Road
Denby Dale, Huddersfield
West Yorkshire HD8 8TH

Sole distributors for the USA
Motorbooks International
PO Box 2
729 Prospect Avenue
Osceola
Wisconsin 54020
United States

Contents

Foreword by Geoff Duke, O.B.E.

When I heard that Denis Jenkinson was putting together a pictorial record of 'Motorcycle Road Racing in the 1950s', I was delighted!

Who better than Denis, so actively involved in motorcycle racing at that time as 'passenger' — not a very apt description to World Sidecar Champion Eric Oliver, THE Maestro on three wheels.

Now that I have had the opportunity of feasting my eyes on this magnificent photographic collection, complemented by the author's own comments, my eager anticipation has been more than justified.

The photographs, most of which I haven't seen before, will serve enthusiasts for our sport as a constant reminder of those 'Golden Years of Motorcycle Racing', when riders, mechanics, technicians, and racing managers achieved greatness more by in-bred enthusiasm, instinct, and ingenuity, than by the computer.

I am reminded of so many great 'Characters' such as, Harold Daniell with his dry sense of humour, Ernie Thomas whose stories had us all in fits of laughter, Walter Zeller, and Alfredo Milani. Also sadness, at the loss, not all through racing, of great riders like Freddie Frith, Artie Bell, Les Graham, and Reg Armstrong, to name but a few. This book abounds with the racing motorcycle designer's art, and it's all in here in pictures!

Recorded also, is the sad occasion at the end of 1957 when the leading Italian factories pulled out of motorcycle road racing and so opened the door to Japanese supremacy. Then, later, the F.I.M. decision to inhibit engine development by limiting the number of cylinders allowed according to the cubic capacity of an engine. Effectively outlawing beautiful, exotic machines like the V-8 Guzzi. Supposedly on the grounds of cost — what price that theory now!

Well done Denis — I shall treasure my copy!

Geoff Duke riding an early 1950s' factory Norton at the 1985 TT.

Introduction

This is a book about the professional international motorcycle racing scene when it reached a peak in the mid-1950s. It deals with the lead-up to this golden age and the decline and fall which followed. European racing was mostly on open-road circuits, street circuits and park circuits, while in the UK racing was confined to small artificial road-type circuits and the Isle of Man, which was a law unto itself.

In 1955 the motor-car racing world suffered a catastrophe at the Le Mans 24-hour race when a car went into the poorly protected spectators, causing a terrible death toll, and the back-wash from this had far-reaching and permanent effects.

The Swiss Government promptly banned all forms of racing in their country, which not only killed off the Swiss Motorcycle Grand Prix, one of the biggest European events, but also put a stop to all the smaller events at places like Lugano, Locarno, Erlen, Olten and many more. Other countries suffered race losses because new and stringent safety measures had to be taken, and in France, Belgium and Holland many of the race meetings had been organized by car clubs, to which motorcycle racing was added as an extra attraction. When these clubs had to abandon their events because they could not afford to comply with the new rules, the motorcycle world was also an unfortunate loser.

It took two or three years for the Le Mans disaster to take effect, but when it did it killed off the old-style road racing and encouraged the building of permanent circuits, though one or two exceptions survived.

What had been happening was that when racing restarted in 1946 it tried to carry on as if the 1939-45 war years had not happened. The aftermath of the war covered up the deficiencies of open-road racing and after six years of total danger from war, safety was of little consequence in the sport. By the mid-fifties a new breed of racing rider and spectator was appearing, who had either not experienced the danger of wartime or had been too young to understand it. The 1955 Le Mans disaster brought it home to them that the world was no longer living in 1939. Added to this, speeds of racing motorcycles had risen dramatically and the consequences of accidents was making people very apprehensive. Thus the mid- to late fifties saw the dawn of 'the brave new world' and was the death knell of old-time, pre-war European road racing.

The British had only experienced such racing in the Isle of Man and Ireland; on the mainland racing had always been restricted to purpose-built circuits like Cadwell Park, Scarborough, Brands Hatch and converted airfields. By the end of the fifties Europe was having to look to 'closed'-circuit racing and follow the lead of the British, a lead forced upon them by government ruling many years ago, and not one that they had wanted.

Racing machinery followed a similar pattern of events; new rules by the *Federation Internationale Motorcycliste* (FIM) after the war set development back a number of years, as is explained in the early chapters, and the early post-war years had a look of the mid-1930s about them. A new breed of machine began to evolve and this coincided with a decline in the British motorcycle industry, so that Italy led the field in solo racing and Germany in sidecar racing. Streamlining, or as we now call it, aerodynamics, took a hold and spread so rapidly that the FIM had to curb the designers' enthusiasm. Riding techniques changed from the neat, stylish and smooth to the effective but untidy style of no longer being 'at one' with the machine. Utilization of tyre adhesion and weight transfer was more important for in-creasing cornering ability. The streamlining of sidecar outfits blossomed in the period covered by this book, and led to the ultimate demise of a racing sidecar being something attached to a solo machine to a three-wheeler unit that in later years became a racing car with a wheel missing.

The 1950s really saw the end of the period that the war interrupted and the dawn of a new age, the one in which we now live.

Denis Jenkinson
Crondall, Hampshire, 1989

Might Have Been

When the war put a stop to international motorcycle racing in September 1939, the scene was on the threshold of a most interesting and exciting part of its history. For years the idea of a racing motorcycle had been a single-cylinder engine in a glorified push-bike frame, and though adventurous manufacturers had experimented with all the obvious innovations, none had really swayed the overall conception of the racing motorcycle. Single-cylinder Norton and Velocette machines had monopolized the Tourist Trophy races in the Isle of Man and at many other less strenuous circuits in Ireland and throughout Europe, but German and Italian designs were gradually changing the scene.

The 'Blue Riband' of racing was the 500cc class, and capacity was the only limitation, there being no restrictions on the number of cylinders or the means of induction, and though supercharging had long been experimented with for Brooklands Track racing by various specialists, it was the German and Italians who forged ahead with supercharging for road racing.

The supercharged B.M.W. flat-twin and the supercharged four-cylinder Gilera were leading the way and by 1939 all the serious factory racing departments were well into multi-cylinders and supercharging. A.J.S. had built a remarkable water-cooled blown V-4, Velocette had a very advanced blown vertical twin, with shaft drive, B.M.W. and Gilera had stabilized their supercharged designs, and Bianchi, Benelli and Guzzi were well into multi-cylinders or supercharging, or both. Until the end of 1938 the factory Norton team of unblown classic single-cylinder bikes and Velocette with their swinging-arm rear suspended 350cc and 500cc singles were still able to challenge the opposition, more thanks to British riders than anything else. Approaching War Department contracts caused Norton to withdraw their works team for 1939, and they lent their 1938 bikes to riders to use as private entrants, but the writing that had been on the wall for a year or two could not be ignored. Germany swept the board in the Senior TT in the Isle of Man with blown B.M.W. twins in first and second places, while Gilera's blown four-cylinder took the very fast Ulster Grand Prix on the Clady circuit.

Velocette had produced their supercharged vertical twin for TT practice and it had shown good promise, while A.J.S. were already race-worthy with their supercharged water-cooled V-4. In the Ulster GP Walter Rusk clocked the first 100 mph lap riding the V-4 Ajay, only to be bettered by Dorino Serafini on the transverse four-cylinder Gilera.

The battle of the blown multis was hotting up and everything looked set for some really exciting Grand Prix racing in 1940, but suddenly all the lights went out and that was that for six long years.

The victory of B.M.W. in the 1939 Senior TT in the Isle of Man was a personal affront to the British racing scene. Winning in strange 'foreign' lands was one thing, but on the Island was something else. Tall, blond Georg Meier surprised a lot of people with his forceful riding of the supercharged 500cc flat-twin from Munich.

This is the right-hand side of the blown twin B.M.W. engine. The Roots-type supercharger is mounted in front of the crankcase. The carburettor is on the right with the inlet pipes passing under the cylinders. Overhead camshafts were shaft driven, and the lever rising from the gearbox is a neutral-selector.

To rub salt into the 1939 TT wound, J. M. 'Jock' West rode another supercharged B.M.W. into second place. He is seen 'standing on the pegs' as he lands rather heavily on the front wheel.

In European races the supercharged water-cooled transverse four-cylinder Gilera gave B.M.W. a hard time. The Italian machine did not race in the Isle of Man in 1939, but it did appear at the Ulster Grand Prix on the very fast Clady circuit and left everyone behind on sheer speed. Dorino Serafini's winning machine is seen in the Ulster paddock being watched over by his pit attendant.

A.J.S. had experimented with multi-cylinders and superchargers for some time, and their 1939 bike showed great possibilities against the Europeans. Their final word before the lights went out over Europe was this supercharged 500cc water-cooled V-4. It was tested at Brooklands by A. R. ('Bob') Foster, hence the ungainly regulation silencers and fishtails on the four tiny exhaust pipes, before going to the Isle of Man for the TT.

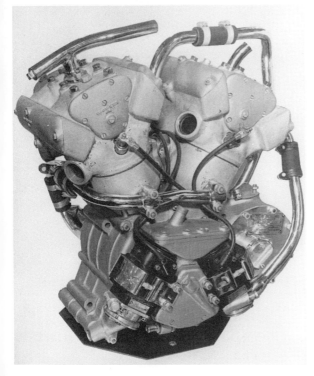

The compact water-cooled V-4 A.J.S. 500cc engine with the supercharger mounted in front, driven by chain from the engine sprocket, with twin magnetos on the right side of the crankcase.

Two A.J.S. supercharged V-4s were entered in the 1939 Senior TT, ridden by Bob Foster and Walter Rusk. The 'blond bombshell' Rusk finished eleventh, and Bob Foster, seen here on the Mountain, finished 13th.

Irishman Walter Rusk was leading the Ulster Grand Prix on the blown 'Ajay' when front fork trouble caused him to retire. He recorded the first 100 mph lap of the Clady circuit before retiring, which was a landmark in motorcycling history, even though the winner Serafini improved on it later in the race.

Velocette's new supercharged vertical twin was not raceworthy by TT time in 1939, so Stanley Woods had to race the old single-cylinder. Try as he might, and here we see him trying at the top of Bray Hill, he could do no better than fourth.

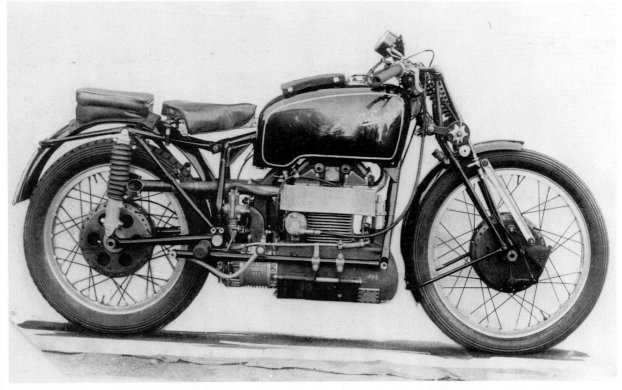

Nicknamed 'The Roarer', the 1939 Velocette supercharged vertical twin 500cc Grand Prix bike was Britain's most likely challenge for honours in 1940. The side-by-side twin had geared-together crankshafts, the right-hand one driving the blower and the left-hand one driving the gearbox. Shaft drive ran through the left-side tubular member of the swinging arm of the rear suspension. This machine was very little bigger than the production 350cc Mk VIII Velocette.

It was not only in the 500cc class that supercharged machines were dominant. In the 350cc class the German D.K.W. team were a force to be reckoned with and Heiner Fleischmann is seen mono-wheeling his supercharged two-stroke water-cooled D.K.W. while racing to third place in the 1939 Junior TT.

Two British riders who saw the potential of foreign machines in pre-war days were E. R. (Ernie) Thomas (left) and E. A. (Ted) Mellors (right), both of whom earned their living racing professionally all over Europe. Mellors rode for Benelli and Thomas for D.K.W. factory teams, as well as racing their own private Velocettes.

The factory 250cc Benelli, with single-cylinder twin-overhead camshaft engine, was a little jewel and this is the bike with which Ted Mellors won the 1939 Lightweight TT in the Isle of Man. Note the forward and rear-set footrests, popular in those days for 'really getting down to it'.

Ted Mellors aviating the beautiful little 250cc Benelli during his winning ride in the 1939 Lightweight TT in the Isle of Man.

If the single-cylinder twin ohc Benelli was a jewel, the 1939 prototype was the crown. This 250cc machine had a transverse four-cylinder engine, with twin ohc, water-cooled *and* supercharged. It was mounted in a similar frame to the single-cylinder machine and was destined to take the 250cc class to new heights, but the war put a stop to it all. Truly a 'might have been'.

In the sidecar racing world one of the first Englishmen, if not the first, to adopt the 'head first, horizontal' position for the passenger was Leslie Seals, riding with A. H. (Arthur) Horton on his Norton outfit. In 1938 they won the sidecar class of the Swiss Grand Prix, a feat that Eric Oliver was to repeat after the war. While normal in European racing, this passenger position caused a bit of a furore among officials in British racing.

Recovery

Hardly had the dust settled on war-torn Europe than racing began again, naturally on a low key compared to where it had left off. Some established circuits were resurrected, while many temporary circuits were laid out on country roads or round the streets of towns. Pre-war there had been a 'hard-core' of private owners who lived by racing all over Europe in the smaller events, with a factory ride here and there in the Grand Prix events. These riders formed the 'Continental Circus', and the likes of Fergus Anderson, Ernie Thomas, Leon Martin, Roger Laurent, the Monneret family and others soon got the ball rolling again.

With racing in Britain restricted to the Isle of Man, Northern Ireland, short circuits on the mainland and aerodrome races, the lure of continental road racing was strong. The regular 'circus' riders were soon joined by Tommy Wood, Dave Whitworth, Jock Weddell, Eric Oliver and many more, while more private owners from Belgium, Holland, Switzerland, Italy, Austria and Spain soon swelled the ranks. Germany was not accepted back into the International Federation to begin with, so they developed their own national scene, using such pre-war machinery that they could scrape up.

For the rest of Europe, Norton, Velocette, A.J.S. and Triumph soon got into production with 'customer' racing bikes, and in Italy Moto Guzzi, Gilera, Mondial, Moto Morini and others were building new racing machinery. The factory Grand Prix scene, so strong in 1939, was strangled at birth by an FIM decision to ban supercharging and the use of petrol/benzole or alcohol fuels. Fuel was limited to low-grade commercial petrol, which was all that was available in most countries. These decisions put paid to any hopes for the Velocette twin and hampered the new A.J.S. twin, which had been designed specifically for supercharging. In Italy Gilera abandoned their water-cooled blown four-cylinder and designed a new air-cooled four, and Benelli abandoned their blown water-cooled four-cylinder. B.M.W., D.K.W. and N.S.U. in Germany were unaffected by this rule change as they could only participate in their national events, so they continued with their supercharged methanol-burning bikes.

Racing in Switzerland was very strong and the Swiss GP had support from all the major factory teams, as there was a lucrative market for the sale of production motorcycles to be influenced by racing successes. The Belgian GP was well supported for the same reasons, as of course was the Tourist Trophy in the Isle of Man and races in Northern Ireland. To begin with many of the factory riders were those who had been at the top in 1939 and had survived the war, and equally most of the private owners had had some pre-war experience, but new names soon began to appear. While the immediate post-war years saw the emergence of new racing machinery it also saw the emergence of new star riders from all the European countries and these were added to by an influx of riders from the British Commonwealth countries. As the pre-war riders began to retire from the scene there was no shortage of newcomers to fill their places.

By the end of the 1940s the international scene had fully recovered and the classic Grand Prix events, which included the Isle of Man TT races, were re-established and supported by the smaller Circuit races. In 1949 the FIM introduced a World Championship series for riders and manufacturers, and this established the 500cc class as the premier category for the factory teams. In the Tourist Trophy the 500cc class, known as the Senior, had always held this position, but now it was officially established in the Grand Prix races in Ulster, Holland, Belgium, Switzerland and Italy.

After a very shaky restart in 1945-46 recovery was now complete.

As soon as racing restarted in a small way in France or Belgium, many riders who had experienced the joys of European road racing in pre-war days were back on the scene with their 1939 bikes. One was M. D. (David) Whitworth, seen here before the start of the 350cc race at Le Zoute in July 1946.

By 1948, Dave Whitworth was an established star in the 'Continental Circus' and is seen here on his new Mk VIII Velocette in the Swiss Grand Prix. Sadly he was to lose his life in the Belgian Grand Prix of 1950.

Was there ever a more professional member of the 'Continental Circus' than F. K. (Fergus) Anderson? He restarted racing in France almost before the dust of war had settled and would race anything, anywhere, at any time. He reached the height of his fame as a factory rider for Moto Guzzi, winning the 350cc World Championship in 1953 and 1954. Here he is seen about to start his 490cc Manx Norton in practice at the Swiss Grand Prix in 1947.

Fergus Anderson smokes his pipe while fettling his 250cc Moto Guzzi 'Albatros' and listens to a Swiss paddock enquirer at the 1948 circuit of Schaffhausen. If Fergus liked you he could not be more helpful; if he didn't like you it was best to go away. The author was honoured to be accepted by his hero.

A pre-war star was Bob Foster, and when he returned after the six-year break he had the same flair and style that kept him at the top of the profession. Here he is in action in the 1947 Ulster Grand Prix on a Mk VIII Velocette.

Members of the 'Continental Circus' came from all over Europe and one French stalwart that got racing going again after the war was the Parisian George Monneret. He brought his two sons into the racing game, and the elder one, Pierre, eventually rode for the Gilera factory team.

A.J.S. produced a brand new post-war 500cc Grand Prix bike, with horizontal parallel-twin engine. One of the first riders for the rejuvenated team was J. M. ('Jock') West, who had finished second in the 1939 TT on a blown B.M.W. Here he is seen cornering during the 1947 Ulster Grand Prix.

Leader of the factory Norton team in the 'recovery' era was bald, bespectacled Londoner H. L. (Harold) Daniell. Not particularly fast on tight hairpins or slow corners, there were few who could equal Harold on a 100 mph full-bore bend, which was where it counted. Seen shaking hands with team-mate A. J. (Artie) Bell after winning the 1947 Senior TT, Harold had on his left tuner Steve Lancefield, Norton MD Gilbert Smith and team-chief Joe Craig.

Belfast rider Artie Bell joined the Norton factory team in the 'recovery' years, and is seen here in the 1947 Ulster Grand Prix on what was basically the 1938 Norton works bike. A big man, Artie was a hard rider of the old school of 'iron men'.

A few bumps, like crossing the tramlines on the Geneva circuit in the 1948 Grand Prix des Nations 350cc event, did not worry Artie Bell.

The recovery years saw many newcomers join the factory teams after giving good performances as private owners. One such was W. R. (Bill) Doran, who rode 350cc and 500cc A.J.S. machines for the Plumstead factory. He is seen 'in his Sunday best' proudly wearing his British Motorcycle Racing Club badge at scrutineering in Belgium.

Bill Doran rounding Governors Bridge hairpin in the 1949 Senior TT on a factory A.J.S. 500cc twin. Not the most stylish of riders, Bill more than justified his place in the team.

If the Dunlop Rubber Company in Birmingham had not gone back into production with racing tyres as soon as it was possible after the war, the years of 'recovery' would have been very hard indeed. Here is their racing-tyre depot in the Isle of Man in 1949.

R. L. (Les) Graham lost the 1949 Senior TT when the magneto drive sheared on his factory A.J.S. twin and he pushed the machine to the finish. Here Artie Bell, of the Norton team, commiserates, while Jock West (in dark glasses) and Reg Armstrong look on.

When the FIM ruled out supercharging in 1947 the Italian Gilera firm produced brand-new machines for the 500cc class, the only similarity being the transverse four-cylinder layout. The new engine was air-cooled and at first breathed through two large carburettors, but later these were replaced by four small ones. Girder front forks were used and swinging-arm rear suspension. This is the 1949 version that was the 'writing-on-the-wall' for all the opposition.

Moto Guzzi were soon back into racing, in spite of the toll of war, and by 1948 were building brand-new machines, both for their own factory team and for sale to acceptable private owners. Their star rider was Enrico Lorenzetti, seen here astride a 1948 'Gambalunga' 500cc single-cylinder, with horizontal barrel, down-draught carburettor and outside flywheel. Note also the very effective bottom-link front forks with long, thin coil springs in the fork legs.

The A.J.S. 500cc parallel twin was originally designed at the end of the war to be supercharged, assuming that things would continue where they had left off in 1939. The ban on supercharging meant that the engine had to be modified to use twin carburettors and run on straight petrol, which hampered its development. Because of the spiky finning on the cylinder heads it was nicknamed 'Porcupine'. It won the first 500cc World Championship in 1949.

The Moto Guzzi 'Gambalunga' was long and low and was particularly good on twisty street circuits. While the factory bikes were painted pale green the private owner machines were invariably Italian red. This is the one that Jean Behra used to become Champion of France in 1949.

Moto Guzzi also made a 250cc version for sale to private owners known as 'Gambalunghino', and here is T. L. (Tommy) Wood finishing second in the 1949 Lightweight TT, which was won by Manliff Barrington on a similar machine.

1948 saw the Eric Oliver/Denis Jenkinson partnership challenging the continentals in the sidecar class with their 596cc Norton with Watsonian sidecar. The passenger normally adopted the horizontal head-first style, but adopted this position for very tight, and slow, hairpin bends. They are seen winning at Zandvoort in Holland.

The two main European adversaries were the Swiss rider Hans Haldemann (No. 18) and Frans Vanderschrick (No. 2) from Belgium. There was no hard and fast rule about which side the 'chair' should be, and while Haldemann is understeering with his passenger over the rear wheel, Vanderschrick is oversteering with his passenger at full stretch. The sidecar outfit is a mechanical phenomenon.

The Swiss rider Hans Haldemann, from Berne, was one of the wiliest sidecar riders and a first-class tuner of Norton engines. He often stretched things a bit too far and suffered engine failures, but seldom if ever made riding errors.

When the FIM introduced the World Championships in 1949 the Gilera factory entered one
of their four-cylinder machines in the sidecar class, to combat Eric Oliver and his Norton.
The works rider Ercole Frigerio is seen on the factory entry at Monza, with his passenger,
Lorenzo Dobelli, and a factory mechanic.

The first World Champion in 1949 was Nello Pagani riding a 125cc Mondial. The very experienced Pagani also rode in the Gilera factory team on their fast four-cylinder bikes, finishing second in the 500cc Championship to Les Graham, and in the same year was racing Maserati Grand Prix cars. He is seen astride a Gilera with Piero Taruffi, the pre-war Gilera rider and engineer.

The 250cc Champion for 1949 was Bruno Ruffo, riding for Moto Guzzi on the 'Gambalunghino'. Bruno did not have an elegant style, but he was a very forceful and urgent type of rider, capable of winning on any type of circuit. He is seen in the Ulster Grand Prix.

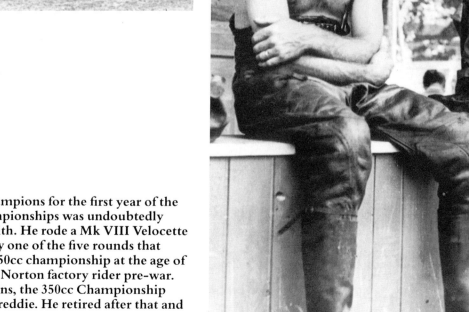

Champion of champions for the first year of the FIM World Championships was undoubtedly F. L. (Freddie) Frith. He rode a Mk VIII Velocette to victory in every one of the five rounds that counted for the 350cc championship at the age of 40, having been a Norton factory rider pre-war. Five races, five wins, the 350cc Championship was enough for Freddie. He retired after that and was later awarded the OBE.

Freddie Frith is seen leading his team-mate Bob Foster across the Eau Rouge river bridge on the fast Spa-Francorchamps circuit during the 1949 Belgian Grand Prix. They finished first and second. Frith had a very distinctive 'lean-out' style of riding.

Freddie Frith was acknowledged to be the ultimate stylist of the 'iron-age' of motorcycle racing. His poise and balance were a joy to watch and personified speed by a professional rider. He is seen in action winning the Dutch Grand Prix in 1949, his last year of racing.

Winner of the 'Blue Riband' of motorcycle racing in the 1949 World Championships was Les Graham on the 500cc A.J.S. Porcupine. He is seen winning the Ulster Grand Prix in his Championship year.

Winners of the first sidecar World Championship were Eric Oliver and Denis Jenkinson, with their Norton/Watsonian outfit. They are seen being congratulated by Championship runner-up Ercole Frigerio.

As the years of 'recovery' come to a close the author is seen with Oliver's Championship-winning Norton sidecar outfit, preparing to load the machine into their Austin 3-Way transport van.

Exodus

In 1950 riders from neighbouring countries were allowed to compete in German events and the following year Germany became fully international. World Championship events were enhanced by entries from N.S.U., D.K.W. and B.M.W., the 250cc class progressing rapidly, with N.S.U. fielding some very advanced machinery, while D.K.W. two-stroke technology entered the 350cc class. B.M.W. were never able to get to grips with the 500cc class, where opposition from Gilera, Moto Guzzi and the new M.V. Agusta were in a class of their own. Only by dint of superior riders were Norton and A.J.S. able to challenge the Italians, so amid this galaxy the Munich flat-twin, now having to run on petrol without the aid of a supercharger, was not in the same league.

Norton had been dominating the sidecar class, but now B.M.W. found their obsolete twin very suitable for the three-wheeler class and eventually took over from Norton.

The early part of the 1950s saw some heroic battles on the circuits of Europe between Italian riders on fast multi-cylinder bikes and British riders on underpowered Norton and A.J.S. machines, and it didn't take long for the British riders to assess the worth of their continental opponents and realize that the future lay in multi-cylinder engines; many a top rider must have followed a screaming Gilera or M.V. Agusta thinking how much faster he could make the Italian machines go. By 1953 the exodus was complete and the Italian factories were using British riders to lead their teams and help in the development of handling and road-holding. Had there been any signs that Norton, Velocette, Triumph or A.J.S. were going to produce equal bikes to the opposition the riders would have stayed, but the British motorcycle industry was in the throes of committing suicide, due to poor management, and there was no future left in Great Britain for top-flight professional riders.

The introduction of the 'Featherbed' Norton frame, with swinging-arm rear suspension, that Velocette had in 1938, rejuvenated the pre-war Norton. With riders of the calibre of the new star G. E. (Geoff) Duke, seen here in the 1950 Grand Prix des Nations at Geneva, the more powerful Italian opposition could be challenged.

The A.J.S. twin was still competitive in 1950, but its future seemed to be limited by its potential for development. Les Graham continued to lead the team, but there seemed to be no long-term future for the Plumstead firm at the top of Grand Prix racing. Les Graham is seen here in the 1950 Senior TT, in which he finished fourth.

The 350cc class was still being dominated by British machines, mainly because none of the European firms had really taken an interest in the class; they were concentrating on the 125cc, 250cc and 500cc classes. The British teams fielded the best riders in the 350cc class, as illustrated here by Artie Bell (Norton) leading Bob Foster (Velocette) in the Belgian Grand Prix in 1950. Sadly, this was Bell's last race. In the 500cc event which followed he was brought off in a multiple accident and his injuries ended his racing career.

A formidable trio: the 1950 Gilera factory team on the powerful four-cylinder 500cc bikes make a fine sight as they corner in formation. The experienced Nello Pagani (1) follows Carlo Bandirola (17) and the rising young Italian star Umberto Masetti (42).

In 1951 Germany was accepted back into the FIM and their factories and riders were able to compete in international events. B.M.W. were soon on the scene with their pre-war star Georg Meier and a stylish newcomer, Walter Zeller. The B.M.W. machines were effectively the 1939 model with the supercharger removed and a carburettor to each cylinder.

B.M.W. had always been keen on sidecar racing, and once back in the FIM a factory entry began to appear ridden by the long-time works rider Ludwig 'Wiggerl' Kraus with Bernhardt Huser in the sidecar. The firm also gave strong support to German private owners, and by the end of 1953 the name B.M.W. was making steady in-roads into the results of the sidecar class, close behind Norton and Gilera.

Outstanding in the 250cc class was the Italian
Benelli firm, racing virtually the same design of
bike that had won the 1939 TT. Their works rider,
Dario Ambrosini, was a tough little Italian who
could really use the lovely little Benelli. On
streaming wet roads he is seen racing to victory
in the 1951 Swiss Grand Prix at Berne.

Dario Ambrosini was the 1950 World Champion
in the 250cc class riding the twin-camshaft
single-cylinder Benelli. In that successful season
he also won the 250cc class in the Isle of Man TT,
and is seen looking very smart in collar and tie
collecting his TT Trophy at the prize-giving. His
meteoric career ended with a fatal crash at Albi
the following year.

The Italian firm of F. B. Mondial had a complete stranglehold on the 125cc class, and their strong little twin-camshaft single-cylinder was a very neat design with the gearbox integral in the crankcase. They won the 125cc championship in 1949, 1950 and 1951 with the Italian riders Nello Pagani, Bruno Ruffo and Carlo Ubbiali.

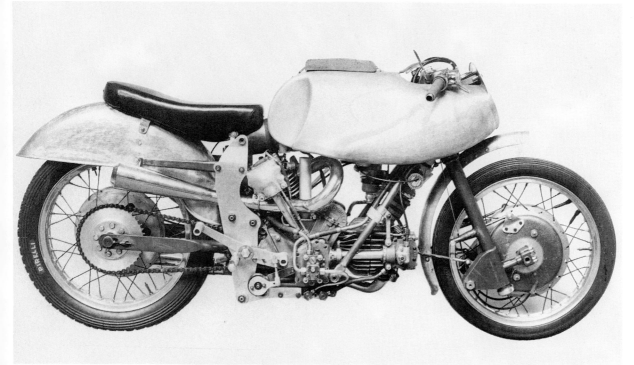

The 500cc Moto Guzzi 120-degree V-twin was a pre-war design which the Mandello firm stretched to its ultimate in development. Light and very fast, reliability was not its strong point, but while the works riders Fergus Anderson, Enrico Lorenzetti and Bruno Ruffo were about with the big-twins, there was no room for complacency. This is the final version as raced by the factory, but already they were designing a replacement.

While the Grand Prix races and the TT were being dominated by the factory teams, the private owners still had plenty of smaller events in which to participate and win. A large field of 350cc bikes is seen getting away in the 1951 Luxembourg Grand Prix, run on a triangular road circuit near the Luxembourg airport.

Winner of the 1951 Luxembourg Grand Prix, a private owners' benefit, was Tommy Wood with his Mk VIII Velocette.

Members of the private-owners 'Continental Circus' travelled all over Europe earning a living from starting money, bonuses and prize money. Two regulars in the early 1950s were C. S. (Sid) Mason and F. P. (Phil) Heath, seen in action in 1951 at a race in Germany.

A German rider who joined the 'Continental Circus' once his country had been accepted back into the FIM was Heinz Thorn-Prikker, seen in action in the 1951 German Grand Prix on his 250cc Moto Guzzi. A large and powerful man, Heinz could tuck himself away on a small bike.

One normally associated the name Tommy Wood with 250cc Moto Guzzi or 350cc Velocette, but here is a rare shot of him winning the Circuit of Erlen in Switzerland in 1950 on a 'Garden Gate' Manx Norton.

Frenchman Jacques Collot won in Madrid on his
500cc Norton . . .

That the 'Continental Circus' travelled far and
wide is illustrated by these three winners.
C. W. (Bill) Petch won at Zandvoort in Holland
on his 350cc A.J.S. . . .

and Ernie Thomas won in Finland on his 350cc
Velocette.

With the superiority of Italian racing engines,
especially in the 500cc class, British riders could
only stand being outclassed by inferior riders for
so long. One of the first to leave a British team
and 'go Italian' was Les Graham, who joined the
recently formed M.V. Agusta team to race their
Gilera-inspired four-cylinder. Les is seen
rounding Ramsey hairpin in the TT in 1951
aboard the 'Italian fire-engine'.

Some riders 'saw the light' as soon as racing got under way after the war, and most notable of these was Fergus Anderson, who was already an established part of Moto Guzzi when the exodus from British teams began.

Those riders who stayed faithful to the cause of British bikes had to ride their hearts out to stay with the Italian machines. None rode harder than Geoff Duke, and he gets his Norton well airborne at Francorchamps while beating the Gileras and Guzzis in the 1951 Belgian Grand Prix, averaging over 106 mph.

Duke again, this time in the 1951 Dutch Grand Prix at Assen, leading Masetti and Pagani on their Gileras in the early stages. Duke was in a class on his own on the works Nortons and won the 1951 'Blue Riband' with victories in the Ulster, Belgian, Dutch and TT races.

Among the Italians there were some 'likely-lads', though they were never quite in the Duke class. One of these was Alfredo Milani, seen in the 1951 Belgian Grand Prix on a Gilera four. He was also an accomplished sidecar rider, though not up to the standard of his brother Albino.

In 1952 Geoff Duke was riding as hard as ever, but to no avail — the Gileras were getting faster all the time and the Nortons were really obsolete by now. As Duke keeps his Norton in the slipstream of Alfredo Milani's Gilera in the fast Belgian Grand Prix he must have been thinking, 'Winning on a Gilera would be easy.'

Among the Italian riders one of the quickest was Umberto Masetti, seen winning the Belgian Grand Prix in 1952 on a works Gilera four. With a further win in the Dutch Grand Prix, and second places to Les Graham's M.V. in Spain and Italy, Masetti won the 1952 500cc World Championship.

Irishman Reg Armstrong persevered with the 500cc A.J.S. twin in 1951 but without success, and after a season with Norton he eventually joined the exodus and 'went foreign'.

59

By 1952 the A.J.S.
'Porcupine' engine was
running out of development
time, even though it had
been improved in detail over
the years. The 'spiky' finning
on the cylinder head had
given way to conventional
finning, but the bike still
retained its nickname.

Many Italian riders graduated into the factory teams, but not all of them were successful, only reaching
the status of 'placemen' rather than winners. Dorino Geminiani was one, who is seen finishing third on
a 500cc Guzzi twin in the 1951 Belgian Grand Prix after faster riders had broken down.

In the Grand Prix races the private owners could not hope to do more than 'make up the numbers', but that did not deter them from having some good dices amongst themselves. Tommy Wood (Norton) leads Jean Behra (Guzzi), George Houel (Gilera Saturno) and Pierre Monneret (Norton) in the 1951 French Grand Prix at Albi. They have just bounced across the level crossing leaving St Jeury.

Two Italian sidecar riders have a private scrap past a café on the Albi circuit during the 1951 French Grand Prix.

European road racing emcompassed all manner of surfaces. Fergus Anderson leads Bruno Ruffo, on their 500cc Moto Guzzi vee-twins, on one of the cobbled streets on the Assen circuit during the 1951 Dutch Grand Prix.

More Grand Prix street racing. Rod Coleman leads Ray Amm, both on Nortons, through one of the villages on the Albi circuit during the 1951 French Grand Prix.

Enrico Lorenzetti changing down with the rocker-pedal foot lever on the factory Moto Guzzi 500cc V-twin during the 1951 Swiss Grand Prix at Berne in very adverse weather conditions.

The original M.V. Agusta 500cc four-cylinder was designed by engineer Piero Remor after he left the Gilera factory team, so the similarity in engine layout was not surprising. However, M.V. Agusta had their own ideas about frames and suspension and after many experiments ended up with an orthodox layout. This is an experimental model for Carlo Bandirola to try in practice for the Swiss Grand Prix in 1952.

Bandirola practising for the 1951 Swiss Grand Prix on an earlier M.V. Agusta with unfaired petrol tank and double-arm rear suspension.

The four-cylinder Gilera was always neater and more efficient-looking than most of its rivals. This 1952 version shows 'English-thinking' on suspension and frame, while the engine relies on short, straight exhaust pipes, unlike English engines, which used megaphone exhaust systems. The sculpted fuel tank shows the beginnings of streamlining.

Rod Coleman, a stylish rider from New Zealand, shows off the classic but dated lines of a works 350cc A.J.S. in 1952. The engine was a breakaway in having three valves for its single cylinder.

The 500cc M.V. Agusta was never a handsome machine, and this version with English 'Earles' front forks was a cumbersome looking brute.

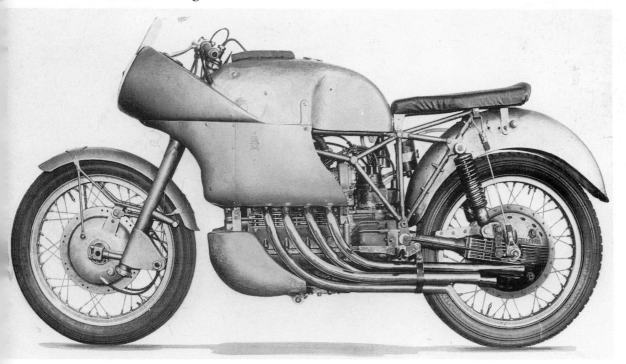

Moto Guzzi replaced their dated 120-degree vee-twin 500cc bike with this very advanced in-line, water-cooled, four-cylinder, with twin overhead camshafts and fuel injection. Shaft drive ran through the left side swinging-arm member of the rear suspension, as it had done on the 1939 Velocette 'Roarer'. The Guzzi engine was a stressed unit, the frame consisting of a small-diameter tubular superstructure. It appeared in late 1952.

The German D.K.W. firm introduced some interest and competition into the 350cc class with an ingenious two-stroke three-cylinder. The engine was transverse with the outer cylinders upright and the middle one horizontal, pointing forwards. The whole machine was very small, very light, very fast very noisy and very fragile. Factory rider Siegfried Wunsche is seen in action in 1952.

From Neckarsulm came the N.S.U. factory team, once Germany was back in the FIM, and they concentrated on the 125cc and 250cc classes. They brought a degree of technical superiority that was awe-inspiring in all things, engine design, suspension, braking and aerodynamics. Although they used some non-German riders at times, there was no shortage of talented riders from the Fatherland. One was Rupert Hollaus, seen aboard a factory N.S.U. in the Dutch Grand Prix.

Italy was never short of interesting motorcycles, though not all of them were successful. This purposeful-looking 250cc Parilla was ridden into fifth place in the 1952 Swiss Grand Prix by its owner, Nino Grieco.

After the death of their rider Dario Ambrosini, the Benelli factory went a bit 'low-key', but returned to the Swiss Grand Prix in 1952 with this new 250cc bike. No official rider was nominated, but at the last moment Les Graham rode it. He finished third, behind the two factory Moto Guzzis of Anderson and Lorenzetti.

The private owners were still hard at it in the Grand Prix races, dicing for minor placings, using the best production racing bikes that were available, though they could not hope to match the works machines. Bill Petch, Ken Mudford and the Belgian 'Erge' have a scrap in Belgium in 1951 on their A.J.S. 7R 'Boy Racers' in the 350cc event.

The Belgian champion Auguste Goffin leads Englishman Les Dear, both on 500cc Nortons, in the 1952 Belgian Grand Prix.

The King abdicates. In May 1953 Geoff Duke went to Monza to try a Gilera four and subsequently signed to ride for the factory team. He is seen talking to Giuseppe Gilera with the test machine, with Alfredo Milani on the right.

Joining the exodus of top riders was Reg Armstrong, riding a 250cc N.S.U. in the 1953 Ulster Grand Prix, which he won. Later he joined Duke in the Gilera team.

As well as racing the 500cc M.V. Agusta 'fire-engine', Les Graham also raced the factory 125cc single-cylinder in the smallest class. He won the 125cc race for M.V. in the 1953 TT, only to crash fatally on the 500cc M.V. in the Senior event.

The double overhead camshaft engine of the 125cc M.V. Agusta factory machine which toppled Mondial from the pinnacle in the 'tiddler class'.

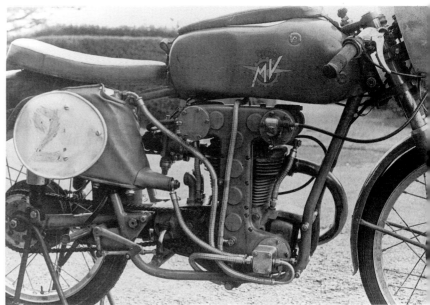

In the smallest class the Italian factories were not short of good home–bred riders. Carlo Ubbiali (M.V. Agusta) and Emilio Mendogni (Moto Morini) were two who rode with distinction.

Streamlining was occupying the thoughts of designers more and more in the search for speed, especially in the smaller categories. In 1953 F. B. Mondial produced this fully faired 125cc model, but it was not the easiest of things to handle in a racing push-start. FIM officials were unimpressed and soon put a curb on such extremes.

The in-line four-cylinder Moto Guzzi was not a success and was soon abandoned in favour of a simpler single-cylinder. They later returned to multi-cylinders with the ultimate racing bike. In 1953 Fergus Anderson rode the four-cylinder at Monza, with full nose-fairing, and the whole bike built lower and smaller than the original one.

Of the Italian riders in the formative years of the Gilera fours, Alfredo Milano was one of the best. He won numerous major events but never a championship.

Moto Guzzi spent much effort on moulding their riders into the motorcycle to cut down wind resistance and drag. The lanky Fergus Anderson was a master at 'getting down to it', as seen in this factory study of him on a 500cc V-twin.

On the 250cc Moto Guzzi, Anderson evolved this method of reducing the frontal area by lifting his legs up out of the wind. The first time he used it, at a French race, officials nearly had a fit, maintaining that he did not have proper control of the machine. A rule was quickly brought in limiting footrest height to no higher than the wheel spindles, and insisting that a rider's feet must always be on the footrests.

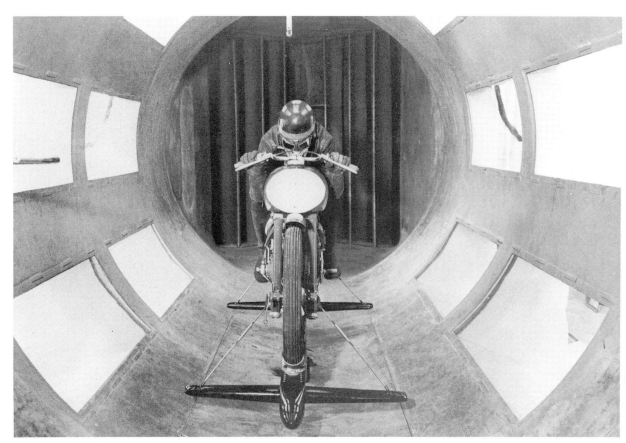

Moto Guzzi had their own full-scale wind tunnel and works riders were encouraged to use it to find the effect of 'sticking their feet or elbows out'. The measured drag was shown on a dial in front of them so that they could see the needle fall back as they raised their head, or even a finger.

Various types of cowling were used by Moto Guzzi. This 'dolphin' style, being ridden by Lorenzetti, was very similar to that introduced by N.S.U.

On the 500cc Moto Guzzi a full nose cowling was used, which became known as a 'dustbin fairing'. These were later outlawed by the FIM for fear that they could restrict steering lock.

B.M.W. experimented with total enclosure streamlining and Walter Zeller rode this rather cumbersome-looking flat-twin in the Italian Grand Prix in 1953.

By the end of 1953 the exodus by top British riders to the Italian teams was complete. This scene in the Italian Grand Prix at Monza of Carlo Bandirola (M.V. Agusta) pursued by Cecil Sandford (M.V. Agusta), Geoff Duke (Gilera) and R. H. (Dickie) Dale (Gilera) says it all. The sound was glorious.

In the sidecar class it was only the brilliance of the riding of people like Eric Oliver and Cyril Smith that kept the Norton/Watsonian outfits ahead of the Italians. Compare this shot of Oliver and Dobelli on the same fast curve as the following photograph.

Ercole Frigerio and Ezio Ricotti on the same fast corner with their four-cylinder Gilera. Note how far out the Italian passenger is having to lean and how the rider is barely off the bicycle. Passenger position is vital to keep 'drag' to a minimum.

Some of the battles between Eric Oliver on his factory-supported Norton/Watsonian outfit against the factory Gilera four-cylinders were memorable. Here he chases Albino Milani at Monza in the 1951 Italian Grand Prix. The Gilera beat the Norton on this occasion by sheer speed.

Eric Oliver stands proudly to attention as the British National anthem is played after he had won the 1951 Belgian Grand Prix sidecar race, assisted by his Italian passenger Lorenzo Dobelli.

Ercole Frigerio was killed when he crashed in the 1952 Swiss Grand Prix at Berne. Not only did the Gilera factory lose a good rider but the sport lost a man who was 'molto simpatico' and liked by everyone, especially his keenest rival, Eric Oliver. This is probably one of the last photos taken of Frigerio in action.

With the Gilera sidecar leader gone it was left to Albino, the eldest of the four Milani brothers, to uphold the firm's honours on three wheels. A ruthless rider, with very little sense of fun, Albino never managed to win a championship.

Hans Haldemann never had the advantage of factory support for his Norton outfit, but was often in the first three by sheer hard riding. The degree of understeer he has on in this picture on the Berne circuit, near his home, is remarkable.

Many of the European riders rode with sidecars mounted on the right simply because that is the way they had learnt to ride an outfit on the road in their youth. Marcel Masuy from Belgium was one of these, and he is seen on the Solitude circuit in Germany with the author as his passenger on their 1952 Norton/Watsonian outfit.

Always an innovator, Eric Oliver produced this fully streamlined Norton/Watsonian sidecar outfit in 1953, preparing for the onslaught by the German B.M.W. outfits that were beginning to show signs of taking over the sidecar class.

Golden Age

With the top riders on the top bikes, especially in the 500cc class, we now witnessed Grand Prix racing of the highest order, and the three Italian factories put everything they had got into racing development. Moto Guzzi also concentrated on the 250cc and 350cc categories, in which they had always been active, while M.V. Agusta, F.B. Mondial and Moto Morini concentrated on the 125cc and 250cc categories, as well as the larger ones.

Apart from the sidecar category, where B.M.W. eventually monopolized, the Italians ruled the roost and the Gilera versus MV Agusta and Moto Guzzi battles for top honours provided some wonderful racing. Streamlining had got a bit out of hand, speed being the obsession, with little regard for practicability or safety and fully enclosed fairings *were the wear*. The FIM were watching developments closely, restricting some technical features on the grounds of safety and rider stability, but none the less the factories forged ahead.

Moto Guzzi led the way technically, and after developing their 120-degree V-twin to its ultimate, they deviated into an unsuccessful in-line four, and then produced what must have been the ultimate racing bike of the golden age. Their 500cc water-cooled V-8 was a complex but intriguing design that set new standards of power and speed, even in its early days of development; it paved the way for a lot of new thinking, and when the others thought about it they realized the enormity of any project to equal it, while Moto Guzzi themselves had stretched their resources to the limit.

By mutual consent the Italian manufacturers, including the smaller-category ones, agreed to call a truce before they annihilated each other both technically and financially. The golden age suddenly stopped at the end of 1957 with a virtual pull-out by the Italian industry.

Gilera were a little cautious in their approach to streamlining, having no small-capacity racing bikes with which to experiment, and Geoff Duke is seen winning the 1954 Swiss Grand Prix at Berne on a partially-faired Gilera four.

Geoff Duke was not only popular in Britain, by reason of his performances on Nortons in the Isle of Man and on the mainland, but all over Europe, especially in Italy, when he took Gilera to World Championships. The Italians called him 'Il Dewkay'.

A promising English lad was W. R. (Bill) Lomas, who joined M.V. Agusta to battle with their cumbersome four-cylinder, and then joined Moto Guzzi and was really heading for the heights when the firm pulled out at the end of 1957. Here Bill is seen having a test-ride on an M.V. four at Monza.

Of the four Milani brothers, Alfredo was clearly the most talented and he stayed faithful to the four-cylinder Gileras for the whole of his professional career. While never a World Champion, he was a strong 'placeman'. He looks pensive as he warms up his bike before the French Grand Prix in 1954, where he finished second to Pierre Monneret on a similar bike.

The 500cc Gilera transverse four-cylinder in 'naked' form was always a thing of beauty, and in this 1954 photo it wears the detachable head fairing and windscreen. It is still on 'straight through' exhaust pipes and uses two-leading-shoe brakes front and rear.

This picture of the N.S.U. factory team warming up before the start of the 250cc race at the 1954 French Grand Prix sums up their domination. The twin-cylinder machines with their distinctive 'dolphin' fairings finished in the first four places, in strict team order. No. 2 (Werner Haas), No. 4 (H. P. Müller), No. 6 (Rupert Hollaus) and No. 8 (Hans Baltisberger).

Bill Lomas did not have much success with the M.V. Agusta four-cylinder, with its leading-link front forks, and when an offer came to join Moto Guzzi he did not hesitate. He looks apprehensive as he aviates the M.V. over Ballaugh Bridge in the Senior TT.

In the 125cc category there were some spirited battles and streamlining was well advanced. Müller's N.S.U. is sandwiched between Copeta and Sandford on M.V. Agustas on the cobbled surface of the Assen circuit in the Dutch Grand Prix. Spectators enjoyed being close to the action in those days.

Werner Haas, the young curly-headed German, was the brilliant leader of the N.S.U. factory team, in 125cc and 250cc categories, and here he shows off the aluminium full-frontal fairing, with perspex screen, during the Dutch Grand Prix in 1954.

Different styles of fairing in the 250cc class are shown by the N.S.U. (No. 3) leading the Moto Guzzi (No. 9) in the 1954 Dutch Grand Prix.

Looking very comfortable and at one with his machine, Geoff Duke speeds on his way to victory in the 1954 Belgian Grand Prix on the fast Francorchamps circuit. He averaged 109.5 mph and was at his best on this type of exacting circuit. Always faithful to his home town of St Helens he wears the Red Rose of Lancashire on his helmet.

Since before the war the Moto Guzzi firm admired the qualities of British and Commonwealth riders and were never slow to recruit them into their ranks. Ken Kavanagh from Australia was a strong member of the team and is seen winning the 350cc class of the Belgian Grand Prix in 1954, on a fully-faired single-cylinder from the Mandello del Lario factory.

N.S.U. domination in the 250cc class is clearly illustrated here in the 1954 German Grand Prix as Werner Haas and Rupert Hollaus race to a 1–2 finish. The 'dolphin' fairings have now given way to the more popular all-enveloping 'dustbin' fairings.

Enrico Lorenzetti's faired-in 350cc Moto Guzzi contrasts vividly with the 'naked' Norton of Jack Brett as they race round the Solitude circuit in the 1954 German Grand Prix.

The poetry-in-motion of Geoff Duke on the Gilera four was renowned. He was undisputed World Champion in 1954 with the machines from Arcore, winning in Belgium, Holland, Germany, Switzerland, Spain and Italy. Here he dives down a sweeping right-hander on the sun-drenched Solitude circuit, during the German Grand Prix.

Geoff Duke (Gilera) leads Ray Amm (Norton) through the sunshine and shade of the return leg of the exciting Solitude circuit near Stuttgart during the 1954 German Grand Prix. They finished first and second.

An heroic rider of the obsolete single-cylinder Norton was Ray Amm from Southern Rhodesia. His riding brilliance kept Norton in the picture beyond all reason. On the long-nosed works machine he won the 1954 Senior TT.

On the 350cc version of Joe Craig's 'long-nose' Norton Ray Amm won the class at the German Grand Prix in 1954 and ended the season with second place in the 350cc and 500cc World Championships. The following year he joined the M.V. Agusta team and was killed at a non-championship race at Imola on a 350cc version of the Italian four-cylinder bike.

British machines without fairings looked very naked during the 'Golden Age' as instanced by Rod Coleman and Bob McIntyre as they race through the streets in the Dutch Grand Prix on their 350cc A.J.S. single-cylinders in 1954.

Gilera often added an extra bike to their regular factory team, and Luigi Taveri is seen having a go on four-cylinder at Monza for the 1954 Italian Grand Prix. He is leading Fergus Anderson on a 500cc Moto Guzzi.

When Geoff Duke won the 1954 Italian Grand Prix he not only settled the World Champion crown for himself, but gave the manufacturer's title to Gilera. A smiling Cav. Giuseppe Gilera, head of the firm, embraces the 'Lad from Lancashire' on the Monza podium.

Eric Oliver and Les Nutt on the streamlined Norton/Watsonian outfit lead the field into the first corner in the 1954 TT on the Clypse circuit. Although they won this race, and the Belgian and Ulster Grand Prix races, they were beaten into second place in the Championship by the more powerful B.M.W. wins.

Winners of the 1954 Sidecar Championships were Wilhelm Noll and his passenger Fritz Cron on their works-supported B.M.W. outfit. Like Oliver/Nutt they won three races, in Germany, Italy and Switzerland, but clinched the title with points gained from second places.

After abandoning their unsuccessful in-line four-cylinder, Moto Guzzi put all their efforts into developing the 500cc Gambalunga model, with great success, but secretly they were designing a new 500cc that was to shake the racing world when it appeared. The Gambalunga, with 'dustbin' fairing, was a beautiful handling bike and Bill Lomas put it to good use in winning the Ulster Grand Prix on the challenging Dundrod circuit in 1955.

The 350cc Moto Guzzi was almost indistinguishable from its bigger brother and was equally handleable on difficult circuits. Ken Kavanagh is seen in practice in the Isle of Man for the 1955 Junior TT.

By 1955 the B.M.W. menace in the sidecar class was strong and Eric Oliver contemplates the situation before the 1955 TT. While battling against the German machines he was forced to retire when his passenger, Eric Bliss, received a bad eye injury from a flying stone.

The 1955 Sidecar TT was a tough event, and Bill Boddice looks somewhat 'knackered' after finishing second, with his passenger Bill Storr. Between them is a very young Mick Boddice, who was to grow up and become as famous in sidecar racing as his father.

The sort of racing that made the fans go wild. Geoff Duke (Gilera, No. 2) and Umberto Masetti (M.V. Agusta, No. 8) are wheel to wheel as they pass the Monza pits during the 1955 Italian Grand Prix. The screaming four-cylinders made the adrenalin flow in everyone who heard them. This dice ended in victory for the wiry young Italian.

As the 1955 season ended Moto Guzzi revealed briefly their new 500cc weapon. A V-8-cylinder engine, with bore and stroke of 44 x 41 mm, mounted transversely in the frame, with eight synchronized carburettors and eight tiny exhaust pipes. It was water-cooled and was so neat and compact that a man could easily pick up the complete power unit. Ken Kavanagh is seen about to start this fantastic machine.

1956 was not a happy season, marred at the beginning by the death of that great professional rider Fergus Anderson. He died in the Circuit of Floreffe, in Belgium, when he crashed his factory B.M.W. twin. After a bad start he had slashed through the field into second place. He is seen on the starting grid of that fateful race, chatting to Jack Brett (Norton, No. 29).

A great set-back to the World Championship scene was Geoff Duke receiving a six-month ban from riding in World Championship events. The FIM dealt this cruel blow to Duke because he had supported a strike by private owners at the 1955 Dutch Grand Prix. Being a factory-paid rider he had nothing to gain, but gave his support for more starting money for the underpaid private riders. He was allowed to compete in non-championship events, and is seen winning the Swedish Grand Prix. Note the Gilera four now sports long megaphone exhaust pipes.

The ban on Geoff Duke left the way open for others, and quick to profit was the rising M.V. Agusta star John Surtees. He won the Senior TT and 500cc Dutch Grand Prix in fine style and this view of him in the Isle of Man shows how his influence at M.V. had tidied up the bike and made it look quite handsome.

Once Surtees had got the big M.V. sorted out to his liking he began to study riding style and developed the system of shifting his weight off the saddle towards the inside of the corner. Not for high-speed corners, where added drag would have been detrimental, but on slow- and medium-speed ones, where the relationship of rider centre-of-gravity to that of the bike showed a gain in cornering power.

Although the 500cc class was M.V. Agusta's all-important objective, they did not neglect the smaller classes, fielding a 350cc version of the four-cylinder and single-cylinder 125cc and 250cc machines. Thi 250cc with 'dustbin' fairing was raced by John Surtees in 1956.

While Moto Guzzi were developing their 500cc V-8, the factory riders continued to race the horizontal single-cylinder bike, with very efficient 'dustbin' fairing.

A stylish rider on a stylish bike was Bill Lomas on the factory 500cc Moto Guzzi, seen in action in the 1956 TT in the Isle of Man.

A man that Moto Guzzi used for development work on their V-8 was the Lincolnshire rider Dickie Dale, an unflappable, safe and knowledgeable rider who was very good at sorting out handling problems. He is seen in the 1956 Senior TT on one of the works single-cylinder machines.

While Bill Lomas chased the more powerful four-cylinder bikes in vain on the single-cylinder Moto Guzzi he couldn't wait to get aboard the new V-8 and race it 'in anger'. Here he is finishing fifth in the 1956 Senior TT.

The Gilera firm sent Geoff Duke away to many far-off places to race and demonstrate their 'fabulous fours', and he is seen riding at Port Elizabeth in South Africa during the 1956 season.

Moto Guzzi were continually probing into aerodynamics in the search for top speed, and Ken Kavanagh is seen testing a fully enclosed single-cylinder 350cc at Monza during 1956. Maximum speed of the 500 versions were becoming 'a bit quick' and aerodynamic stability was very critical. This style of enclosure was not very practical for 'run-and-bump' starts.

'Naked' machines were still part of the scene, and B.M.W. reverted to basics for Walter Zeller's 500cc twin in the Senior TT, in which he finished fourth.

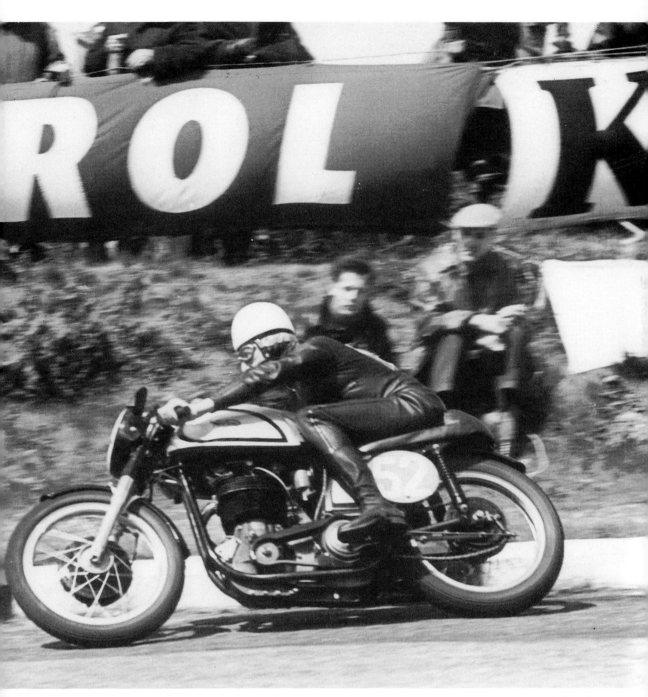

While the factory Norton team had long since withdrawn the firm continued to build racing bikes for sale, and the 350cc and 500cc 'Featherbed' models were the mainstay of private owners, especially in the TT. Performances such as John Hartle's second place in the 1956 Senior TT was the sort of thing that provided a chance of joining an Italian factory team. He later joined John Surtees in the M.V. Agusta team.

A man who fell in love with the phenomenal performance of the V-8 Moto Guzzi was Bill Lomas. Here he is seen being push-started to do some test-riding in the wet in 1956. Note the new-style fairing necessitated by the need for a lot of air to the water radiator mounted behind the front wheel. During some record attempts he was timed at over 175 mph.

A stylish and consistent rider was the German Walter Zeller on the factory B.M.W. twin, here seen in its 1956 form, with leading-link front forks. He finished second in the 500cc World Championship behind John Surtees.

Even the mighty can fall! Geoff Duke sliding away from his Gilera four after crashing in the early-season non-championship race at Imola in 1957. After his suspension in the first half of 1956 he stormed back into contention in the Belgian Grand Prix, leading the M.V. Agustas until his Gilera engine broke a valve. At Monza he won the Italian Grand Prix, showing he had lost none of his touch. This aberration at Imolas put him out of all but two of the 1957 Championship events.

With Duke side-lined for most of 1957 it seemed that John Surtees would have a clear run on the much improved Gallerate 'fire-engine' from the Meccanica Verghera factory, seen here in 1957 form with sculpted petrol tank for the rider to fit into, but it was not to be.

New Zealander Bob Brown was another 'iron man' recruited into the Gilera team to ride both the 350cc and 500cc versions. He is seen on the 350cc bike riding to third place in the 1957 TT.

Gilera strengthened their team, now fielding 350cc and 500cc fully-faired versions of their four-cylinder bikes, by the addition of the rugged Scot Robert Macgregor McIntyre, who won the 350cc and 500cc TT races for them. Was there ever a more forceful and determined rider than 'Bob Mac'?

Although the 350cc four-cylinder Gileras and M.V.s were having some good scraps among themselves, it was often for second place, as the unobtrusive Australian Keith Campbell was piloting his works Moto Guzzi into first place to become 350cc Champion in 1957. This impressive view of him in Swede assumes that he had done domething about the chalked instructions on his fairing which reads 'No oil — Senza olio!'

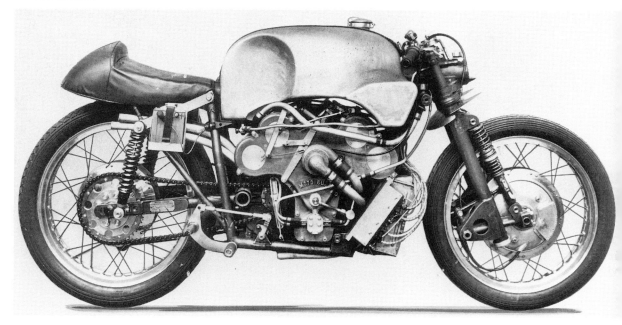

While Gilera and M.V. Agusta were dominating the 500cc class in 1957 they had to continually keep an eye over their shoulders for the V-8 Moto Guzzi, here seen in all its mechanical complexity without its fairing.

Dickie Dale rode the enclosed Moto Guzzi V-8 into fourth place in the 1957 TT, in spite of the engine firing on only seven cylinders for much of the time. These initial forays had the opposition wondering what they were going to be able to do about this fantastic machine in 1958 once it was fully sorted out.

Such were the battles among the 'big boys' during 1957 that the other classes almost got overlooked. Development continued apace in the 125cc and 250cc classes and a new star, who won the smallest championship class, was Tarquinio Provini riding for Mondial. He was also runner-up to his team-mate Cecil Sandford in the 250cc championship. On this 250cc Mondial with full enclosure he was leading the Belgian Grand Prix until mechanical trouble put him out on the last lap.

1957 ended on the highest note imaginable with a Gilera 1-2-3 in the Italian Grand Prix at Monza and M.V. Agusta 4-5-6. Twenty-four tiny cylinders in unison on full song, a wonderful sound. Here Duke just pips Alfredo Milani for second place, behind the new Italian star Libero Liberati. Surtees, Masetti and Terry Shepheard followed them home on the M.V. Agustas.

Libero Liberati in action at the start of his Gilera four career, when he won the Italian Championship in 1955. Two years later, as the 'Golden Age' came to an end, he won the German, Ulster and Italian 500cc Grand Prix events and was second in the Dutch Grand Prix, taking the World Championship from Bob McIntyre and John Surtees.

Libero Liberati, the 1957 World Champion in the 500cc class, riding for Gilera. The sudden pulling out by the Gilera factory put paid to his career.

The fabulous four–cylinder Gilera which dominated the 'Golden Age' of Grand Prix racing, winning the 'Blue Riband' in 1950, 1952, 1953, 1954, 1955 and 1957.

Withdrawal

True to their word Gilera, Moto Guzzi, F.B. Mondial and Moto Morini all withdrew their factory teams, but M.V. Agusta changed their mind and continued to race their four-cylinder bikes in 350cc and 500cc form, and their single-cylinders in the 125cc and 250cc categories. Opposition was virtually non-existent and it was not unusual for M.V. Agusta to win all four categories at a Grand Prix meeting.

None of the factory machinery of 1957 was made available when other teams were withdrawn, so all the private owner could do was to race 'production racing bikes' built by Norton, A.J.S. and Matchless from England or B.M.W. Rennsport production racers from Germany. All that the works M.V. riders had to do on the four-cylinders was to ride fast and carefully and finish, they never had to do open

battle with any serious opposition, which was a far cry from the previous year or two.

It was a pity that M.V. Agusta did not enter the sidecar class, for then they could have made a clean sweep of all the championship classes, always assuming they could have beaten B.M.W. The low centre of gravity and good torque of the Munich flat-twins seemed tailor-made for sidecar outfits and while they monopolized this category, as M.V. Agusta were doing in the 350cc and 500cc solo classes, the outcome depended on the rider and passenger, for though it was effectively a 'one-make' category, anyone could win.

The high point that racing had reached at the end of 1957 carried the interest through to 1958, and it was not until the end of the season that the full impact of the Italian withdrawal was really appreciated.

Before the 1958 season began M.V. Agusta made it quite clear that they had no intention of withdrawing from racing. An early test-session at Monza saw a formidable line-up. Left to right, Remo Venturi (350/4), Carlo Ubbiali (250 single), Tarquinio Provini (125 single) and John Surtees on a new and experimental 500cc transverse six-cylinder.

The riders that were 'laid-off' by the withdrawal of factory teams had to look elsewhere and some unusual combinations of rider and machine were seen. None was more so than Geoff Duke on a works 500cc B.M.W. flat-twin. Although Duke tried hard to come to grips with the Munich machine, he was never very successful and soon looked elsewhere.

While the 350cc and 500cc classes became a one-factory monopoly the 'tiddlers' still provided some fast and close racing. Luigi Taveri (Ducati) leads Carlo Ubbiali and Tarquinio Provini (M.V. Agustas) in the 125cc class of the Dutch Grand Prix.

The 'Tiddler' racing was further enlivened by the entry of the M.Z. firm from East Germany.
These highly developed two-stroke machines were more than capable of challenging the Italian
twin-overhead camshaft four-stroke bikes, in both the 125cc and 250cc classes. The 125cc M.Z. team
are seen at the Ulster Grand Prix in 1958.

Knowing John Hartle's ability from his Norton days, John Surtees was very happy to have him as his number two in the M.V. Agusta team. While Surtees stands on the podium wearing the winner's laurels after the 350cc event at the Dutch Grand Prix, Hartle is one rung down, probably wondering when it will be his turn to be on the top rung.

While M.V. Agusta were monopolizing the 350cc and 500cc solo classes, B.M.W. had a stranglehold on the sidecar class, so much so that one or two championship meetings dropped the three-wheeler category from their programme. The Belgian Grand Prix was always faithful to the 'chairs' and Walter Schneider is seen leading Florian Camathias round La Source hairpin on their B.M.W. outfits, the German adhering to a right-hand sidecar and the Swiss preferring a left-hand one.

During this first year of lack of real interest in the 500cc class there were interesting things happening in the smaller classes. One of these was the appearance of S. M. B. Hailwood, a 19-year-old who finished third in the 250cc TT race on the short Clypse circuit on a production-racer N.S.U. It is doubtful whether anyone realized at the time just how far Mike Hailwood would go in the coming years.

The M.V. Agusta team provided their own opposition and sometimes it was hard. In the Senior TT John Hartle had to abandon his 500/4 when it caught fire due to a split petrol tank. He was lying second to Surtees at the time and is seen beyond the burning bike, keeping well clear of the inferno.

John Hartle in action on an M.V. Agust 500cc four-cylinder in the Belgian Grand Prix of 1958. He did not have the best of luck with the Italian team, this time finishing third after a pit stop lost him two minutes over Surtees, who had another runaway win. In second place was ex-Moto Guzzi rider Keith Campbell on a private Norton.

With no factory pay-roll to sustain them the ex-works riders had to take every opportunity to race, and sadly Keith Campbell lost his life in a small French event at Cadours. He won the 350cc event and was leading the 500cc event when he crashed.

Behind the all-conquering four-cylinder M.V. Agusta team there were some varied scraps. In the Italian Grand Prix at Monza, Bob Anderson (Norton) leads Gerhard Klinger (B.M.W.), John Hartle (Experimental M.V. six) and Geoff Duke (Norton). The six-cylinder M.V. Agusta retired when the engine suddenly died.

Low Point

Racing declined into the doldrums, where if M.V. Agusta did not enter it wasn't much of a race; no matter who won, and some very good riders did win, the result could not be regarded as more than clubman's racing. The works M.V. Agusta riders merely had to race against themselves and make sure they did not fall off or blow up the machinery. The Italian factory dominated the 350cc and 500cc classes with their 'fire engines', as the red machines became known. Some events went so far as to drop the 350cc category, viewing it as not worthwhile as it was only a repetition of the 500cc race.

In the smaller classes the East German M.Z. factory team and the Italian Ducati factory gave M.V. Agusta some opposition, but at the end of the season it was M.V. that won all the solo championships.

Before the 1950s were out a light appeared in the east, with entries in the smaller classes by Japanese manufacturers; a Honda finished sixth in the 125cc race at the Tourist Trophy in the Isle of Man. In the doldrums that the Italian withdrawal had created these tentative probes from Japan did not appear significant, but in the following decade they changed the face of motorcycle racing the world over. But that is another story.

Among the riders who had risen to the top with the Gilera team was Bob McIntyre and after the withdrawal he had little option but to return to basics and ride production racing Nortons. Though no longer able to challenge the M.V. Agusta team, 'Bob Mac' was still a joy to watch and his riding was as purposeful and forceful as ever. He is seen finishing fifth in the 1959 Senior TT.

Prior to the Tourist Trophy races in the Isle of Man in 1959 a team of Japanese riders and machines arrived at London's Heathrow airport. They were (bottom to top) Giichi Suzuki, Junzo Suzuki, Naomi Taniguchi and Tiesuke Tanaka. Their machines were twin-cylinder 125cc Hondas. The Japanese invasion had begun.

Giichi Suzuki is seen practising in the Isle of Man on his 125cc Honda. In the race he finished seventh, while his team-mate, Naomi Taniguchi, was just ahead in sixth place. Many people dismissed this first sighting of the Japanese as unimportant, saying that they had a lot to learn. It did not take them very long to learn!

In the small-capacity class M.Z. were still giving the Italians a good run and the competition between them was so intense that they did not really have time to look over their shoulders at the Rising Sun. Luigi Taveri, from Switzerland, had left Ducati and joined the East German team.

Taveri's departure from the Italian Ducati team left a gap, but this was quickly filled by Mike Hailwood, to start a relationship that was to endure for many years. It started Hailwood on the path to the top of the tree, regardless of engine size, make of machine, type of circuit or conditions. To the world in general he was to become quite simply 'Mike the Bike'.

The first three in the 1959 TT for 125cc machines should not have been looking at the camera, they should have been looking over their shoulders at the Rising Sun. Centre is Tarquinio Provini, the winner on an M.V. Agusta, on the right is Luigi Taveri, second on an M.Z., and on the left is Mike Hailwood, third on a Ducati.

Leader of the East German M.Z. team was Ernst Degner, a talented rider whose main objective apart from winning was to defect from behind the 'Iron Curtain'. He sits astride his works M.Z. on the starting grid before the Ulster Grand Prix in 1959.

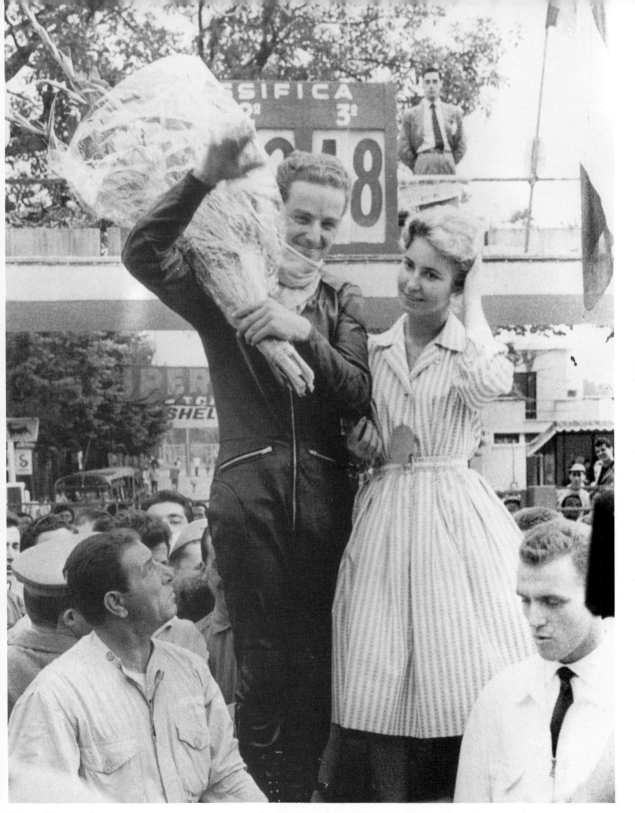

Ernst Degner's greatest moment came at the Italian Grand Prix in 1959, when he won the 125cc event, beating the Italians on their home ground and M.V. Agusta virtually on their own doorstep. Accompanied by his girlfriend, he acknowledges the plaudits of the crowd, while the man on the left looks on in disbelief that M.V. Agusta had been beaten.

Sidecar racing continued to be dominated by B.M.W. at the end of the 1950s, ridden principally by German and Swiss riders. Florian Camathias, with his passenger Helmut Cecco, from Switzerland, sweep past an Isle of Man shop on their way to second place behind World Champion Walter Schneider in the 1959 TT.

Nothing could stop John Surtees on the four-cylinder M.V. Agustas and in 1959 he won every 350cc and 500cc World Championship event on the Italian 'fire-engines' to become World Champion in both categories. He is seen winning the 1959 Senior TT.

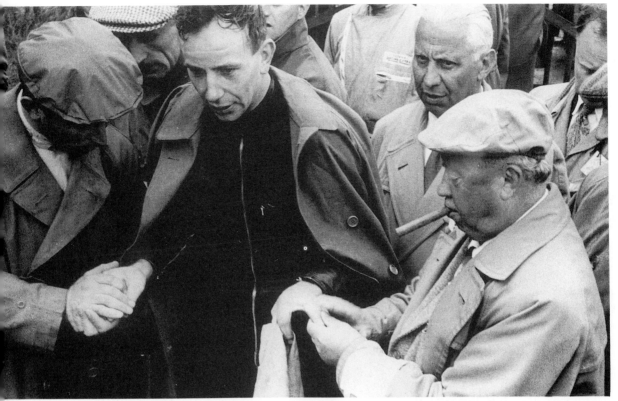

John Surtees did not win all his races with ease, for though there may not have been any mechanical opposition to the M.V. Agustas, he had to battle against the elements at times. He is receiving attention to his frozen and numb hands after winning the 1959 Senior TT at an average speed of 87 mph in the most awful wet and cold conditions imaginable. His speed was 11 mph slower than his victory the previous year.

By the end of the season M.V. Agusta promoted Remo Venturi from their small-capacity bikes to the 350cc and 500cc four-cylinder machines. Venturi is seen having a test-ride on a four-cylinder at Monza.

While John Hartle rode the experimental six-cylinder M.V. Agusta at the end of the season, Surtees and Venturi ended the 1950s with a clean sweep for the Gallerate firm. Riding the four-cylinder bikes they finished first and second in the 350cc race, and first and second in the 500cc race in the Italian Grand Prix meeting at Monza. Winner Surtees, in the centre, welcomes his team-mate on the winner's rostrum.

Records

With racing tied in with sales, motorcycle manufacturers liked to be able to promote racing successes at the annual Motor Cycle Shows, so it became traditional to end the season of Grand Prix racing with a bout of record-breaking.

These record attempts were made with Grand Prix machinery suitably modified for the occasion, over short distances where speed or time was impressive on the advertising panels. The banked track at Montlhéry in France was a popular venue, as was the fast Monza circuit in Italy, or on roads specially closed for the occasion.

If your racing motorcycles had won the World Championship it was nice to add the kudos of the claim to be the world's fastest in some internationally accepted category over a fixed distance. This all helped to establish your production bikes as direct descendants of the Championship bikes, even if only the name on the tank was the same.

During the period under review there were some interesting record attempts, some of which are depicted in this final chapter.

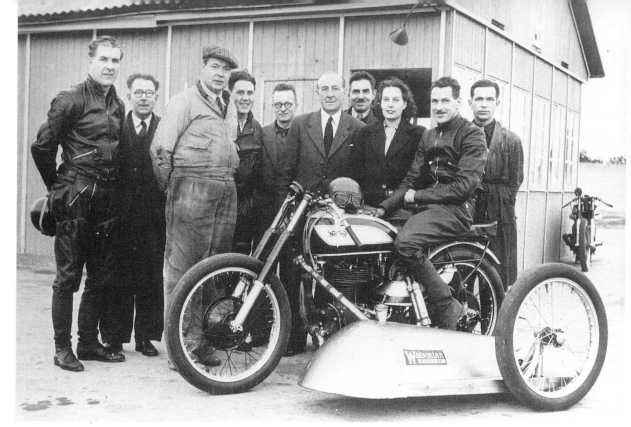

At the end of the 1949 season the Norton team went to the Montlhéry banked track near Paris to set up new solo and sidecar records. Eric Oliver sits on his works-prepared Norton with special Watsonian sidecar containing a long-range fuel tank. In the group (left to right) are Artie Bell, Ron Watson of Watsonian sidecars (in cap), Geoff Duke, Joe Craig in centre, M. Garreau (French Norton importer) and, far right, Charlie Edwards, Norton racing mechanic.

A.J.S. were also frequently seen on the banked Montlhéry track with the 500cc Porcupine and various versions of the 350cc 7R Boy Racer. They hitched a third wheel to a works 350cc solo bike to enable Frenchman George Monneret to attack sidecar class records.

In 1952 the A.J.S. works team had a bout of solo record breaking with their 3-valve 350cc machine. George Monneret is about to set off watched by son Pierre and works rider Bill Doran.

In Italy Fergus Anderson is seen on a Moto Guzzi 500cc vee-twin attacking standing-start mile records on a closed public road. Note the Anderson casual approach to record runs, wearing overalls and tennis shoes!

Another bout of record breaking at Montlhéry by the works Norton team saw Ray Amm riding the fully-streamlined Norton with 'kneeling' riding position. He is making a pit stop for a new rear wheel and tyre during a long-distance run. The Avon technician is on the right with the new wheel and tyre, accompanied by an FIM observer.

The loneliness of the World Record breaker is typified by this late afternoon shot of Dickie Dale on a 350cc Moto Guzzi with third wheel attached. The scene is the Montlhéry track in mid-November 1955.

As Wilhelm Noll prepares for a record run on the Munich-Ingolstadt Autobahn, specially closed for the occasion, he is encouraged by some famous German speed men. On the left is Georg Meier, 1939 TT winner, on the right is World Speed Record holder Ernst Henne, and in the middle is sidecar ace Wiggerl Kraus. Noll achieved a speed of 174 mph with the regulation third wheel attached.

The tension at the start of a record run is shown in this photo of Bill Lomas as he lets in the clutch on a 500cc V-8 Moto Guzzi. He is about to attack the standing-start 10-kilometre record. It was on these runs that the V-8 Guzzi in Grand Prix trim was timed at over 175 mph in 1957.

In the final year of the 1950s the Swiss rider Florian Camathias attacked sidecar records with a works-sponsored B.M.W. The 'wheel-on-a-stick' constituted a regulation sidecar and passenger weight took the form of lead ballast in the streamlined pod by the wheel.

Gilera had an absolute orgy of record breaking at Monza before finally closing down their racing department. Works riders Romolo Ferri, Alfredo and Albino Milani and Bob McIntyre set up records with 125cc, 175cc, 350cc and 500cc solo machines, and with a third wheel attached to the 350cc and 500cc Gilera fours. Among them Alfredo set a standing-start kilometre in 20.95 seconds on the 500/4.

The fully-enclosed Gilera 500/4 had a third wheel attached to it with tubes going through the fairing and Albino Milani averaged over 116 mph for the 1-hour record.

Bob McIntyre being push-started on the 350cc four-cylinder Gilera at Monza during the factory record session. He set an all-time record, regardless of engine capacity, for 1 hour with a speed of 141 mph round the banked track. It was a fitting close to Gilera's ten years of post-war racing and record breaking.